Space Camp

Written by Sarah O'Neil

Illustrated by Pat Reynolds

Flying Start
to Literacy®

Contents

Chapter 1

Room mates

"Wow!" said Calvin, as he charged into the room. "You've already got your space overalls on. Where do I get mine?"

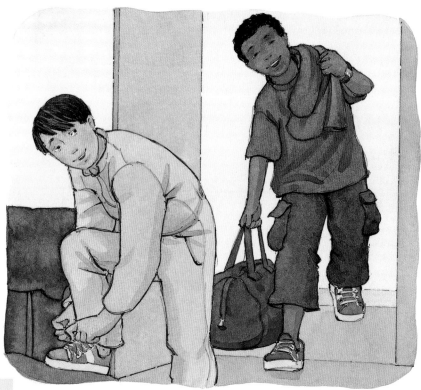

"They're in your cupboard,"
said Mark.

"I'll put them on while you read
out what we are going to do
at space camp," said Calvin.

"Well," said Mark, "today at
dinner we get to eat space food."

"Fantastic," said Calvin. "I can't
wait to try space food. I wonder
what it tastes like."

"And then each day we get to do
the same things that astronauts do,"
said Mark.

"Look at this," said Calvin, looking over Mark's shoulder. "Tomorrow we do a special activity."

"What is it?" asked Mark.

"We get to see what it is like when an astronaut works outside the space station. In space, things float around as if they have no weight."

"How do we do that?" asked Mark.

"We have to build something under water – at the bottom of a deep swimming pool," said Calvin. "Working under water is like working in space."

And that was when Mark's heart sank.

Chapter 2

That sinking feeling

Mark was a very good swimmer. He could dive to the bottom of the pool and pick things up, but only in water where he could stand up.

When Mark thought about going under all that cold, dark water it made him shake inside.

"What's the matter?" said Calvin. "Don't you want to do the underwater challenge?"

"I do," said Mark, as he wiped his sweaty hands on his pants. "Oh, yes, I really want to, but ..."

Calvin looked at his watch. It was dinner time.

"Come on," he said. "Let's go and get our dinner."

Mark and Calvin ate space food for dinner. Some of their food, like apples and potatoes, was the same as everyday food. But some of the food was very different.

"Wow," said Calvin. "I like this freeze-dried ice-cream."

But Mark wasn't very hungry. He couldn't stop thinking about the underwater challenge in the morning.

All night he tossed and turned – he couldn't sleep.

Chapter 3

On the edge

The next morning all the kids met Darren the activity leader beside the pool.

"Today," said Darren, "each team has to build a tower at the bottom of the pool from blocks that are very heavy. These are the blocks you will be using."

Calvin and Mark tried moving the blocks but they were too heavy to lift.

"The blocks will be much easier to move in the water," said Darren. "That's because the water supports them. Moving things in the water is a lot like working in space."

Mark stood on the side of the pool.
He looked into the deep dark water.
He wanted to jump in like the
other kids, but he couldn't bring
himself to do it.

"Don't worry," said Darren.
"Even real astronauts are afraid
sometimes."

"No, they're not," said Mark.
"Astronauts are brave."

"Maybe," said Darren.   "But
being brave is not about how
you feel, it's about what you do."

As Mark sat on the side of the
pool and watched the other kids,
he became more and more miserable.

Chapter 4

Watch out!

"All that swimming has made me very hungry," said Calvin, as they headed for the dining room for lunch. Suddenly he stopped.

"Oh, no," he said. "I've left my watch beside the pool. Let's go back and get it."

When they got to the pool there was no one around.

"There it is," said Calvin.

As he ran over to the edge of the pool, he slipped. He hit his head on the side of the pool and fell in.

Down, down, down Calvin sank –
all the way to the bottom of the pool.
He didn't move.

Mark ran to the edge of the pool.
"Help! Help!" yelled Mark.
"We need help in here."

But no one came.
Calvin was drowning.

Mark knew he was the only person
who could save Calvin, but his legs
wouldn't move. Mark felt terrified.
His heart was pounding and he was
breathing very fast.

Then Mark kicked off his shoes.
He took a breath and dived into
the pool. Down, down, down he
swam into the deep, dark water.

Mark grabbed Calvin by the shirt and pushed off from the bottom. Kicking his legs as hard as he could, Mark swam to the surface, pulling Calvin with him.

As Mark's head broke the surface of the water, he saw Darren running towards the pool.

"Help!" he called.

Darren reached over and pulled Calvin out of the water. He thumped Calvin on the back. Then Calvin began to cough.

Chapter 5

In the swim

Calvin was taken to hospital
because he had hit his head.
But he was not hurt badly and was
soon back at the space camp.

"You saved me," Calvin said
to Mark. "You really were afraid
of the deep water, but you jumped
in and got me out. You're brave
and you're a hero, just like
a real astronaut."

"I don't know about that,"
said Mark.

"But," said Mark, "I do know that tomorrow I am going into the pool."

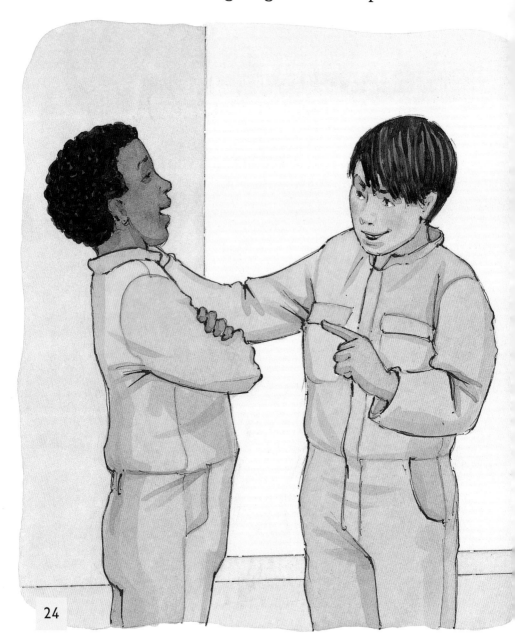